Snake
Detective

Rob Waring, *Series Editor*

HEINLE
CENGAGE Learning™

Australia • Brazil • Japan • Korea • Mexico • Singapore • Spain • United Kingdom • United States

D0584511

Words to Know

This story is set in the Sultanate of Oman, a Middle Eastern country on the Arabian Sea.

A **Snake Detective.** Read the paragraph. Then write the correct <u>underlined</u> word next to each definition.

Gerry Martin is a <u>herpetologist</u> who enjoys solving mysteries about snakes. In this story, he travels to an animal park in Oman to find <u>clues</u> as to why the snakes there are dying. While working with the snakes, he must be extremely cautious, as some of these <u>reptiles</u> can be dangerous. Some of these cold-blooded animals are so <u>venomous</u> that they can kill a person with a single bite. If there's no access to <u>antivenom</u>, the person can die in minutes.

1. a biological product used to treat poisonous animal bites: _____
2. full of a poisonous liquid that certain snakes and insects produce: _____
3. an expert in animals such as snakes and frogs: _____
4. things or facts that help solve a mystery; evidence: _____
5. a group of cold-blooded animals that have backbones, live on land, and usually produce young by laying eggs: _____

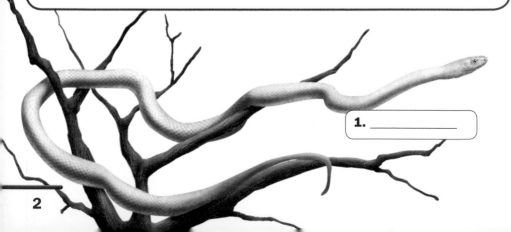

1. _____

B **Dangerous Snakes!** Read the descriptions of some types of snakes found in the story. Then label the pictures with the correct names.

The albino python [ælbaɪnoʊ paɪθɒn] is a very large white snake that wraps itself around its victims.

The cobra's most recognizable feature is the part of its neck that it can flatten outwards in a threat display to appear bigger.

The green mamba is a slim green snake that moves very fast.

The rattlesnake has a noisy tip on its tail used to warn off threats.

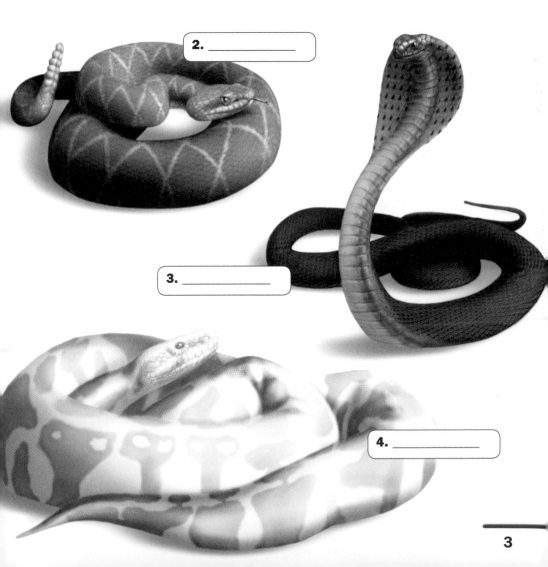

2. _____

3. _____

4. _____

Snake expert Gerry Martin is an Indian herpetologist with a talent for uncovering clues and solving mysteries. When a new challenge to solve a mystery concerning snakes arises, Gerry's always eager to jump at the chance and get on the case. One day, Gerry receives an urgent call from over 2,250 kilometers* away. The caller is a wealthy **sheikh**[1] in the Middle Eastern country of the Sultanate of Oman whose snake park is in desperate need of rescue. As the two men speak on the phone, the sheikh explains the problem. "So you say you've lost all the snakes?" Gerry asks the sheikh as he takes some notes on the case. "How many snakes was that? Over a hundred and forty?" Gerry is amazed. That's a lot of dead snakes, but Gerry is more concerned with something else: What's killing them? And more importantly, how can it be stopped?

Gerry's worries become even greater when he hears the sheikh's next plans. "Okay, so you're planning on getting some new snakes?" replies Gerry when he learns that the sheikh wants to reopen the park in two weeks. If Gerry's going to solve the mystery of the snakes' deaths, he needs to act fast before the new snakes suffer the same misfortune. It's time for a visit to Oman.

_____

[1]**sheikh:** the head of an Arab nation, tribe, or village
*See page 32 for a metric conversion chart.

🎧 CD 2, Track 03

Gerry enthusiastically packs a bag and prepares to travel to Oman, taking with him his reference books on giant snakes as they may help his investigation. Gerry's looking forward to discovering more about the case—and hopefully deducing what the problem is so he can solve the mystery.

When Gerry arrives in Oman, he meets the sheikh whose snake park is in trouble. **Sheikh Amer al-Suleimani**[2] loved the idea of financing a snake park to educate the people of his country about wildlife, but he didn't fully appreciate how difficult it would be to create this type of reptile reserve in the desert. Now he's a bit upset because all of the snakes have died, seemingly for no reason.

The snake park originally housed over 140 snakes from all around the world. But after just a few months, only one snake is still alive, and now Gerry has to find out what happened. He starts his investigation by inspecting the **enclosures**[3] that accommodated the snakes. Gerry then gets the chance to meet the only snake in the park. As he waits nearby, one of the employees of the park quietly walks up with a huge yellowish-white snake **slung**[4] dramatically over his shoulders—it's an enormous albino python. "This one's beautiful. It's lovely," comments Gerry as he reaches out to touch the unusual creature. "It's an albino python." The python may be lovely, but it's the only snake left in the park. It's time for Gerry to find out exactly what's going on.

---

[2]**Sheikh Amer al-Suleimani:** [ʃeɪk ɑmɛər æl suleɪmɑni]
[3]**enclosure:** a small area with a wall or fence around it to prevent escape
[4]**sling:** throw lightly or carelessly

While the sheikh finances the project, it's **Muhammad al-Harthy,**[5] the general manager of the park, who handles the snakes. Muhammad, a real snake enthusiast, describes his long and intense interest in the reptiles. "From [the age of] four years old, I [started] playing with the snakes. Even in school, people used to call me 'snake.' It's [been] my favorite business [since] I was young."

But unfortunately, Muhammad made a mistake when he hired two so-called snake experts from Southeast Asia to help set up the park. Unfortunately, they were not what they appeared to be at all and their input was actually harmful to the snakes. Gerry eventually deduces that it was inevitable that the snakes would die considering the kind of treatment they received from the 'experts.' "Everything they did was wrong. It was painfully wrong. They used to **grab**[6] the snakes with **nooses,**[7] stuff food down their throats, everything that you could possibly do if you wanted to kill a snake."

---

[5] **Muhammad al-Harthy:** [mʊhæməd æl hɑrθi]
[6] **grab:** take quickly and often roughly
[7] **noose:** a rope tied in a circular manner for the purpose of hanging someone by the neck, or holding an animal

After questioning the witnesses, Gerry's next priority is to inspect the scene of the crime. Clue number one is the extremely hot sun and the heat in the desert. Temperature fluctuations of even a few degrees can be harmful to snakes since they are cold-blooded and depend upon the sun to adjust their body temperature. They have a very limited ability to compensate for environmental temperatures above or below their most favorable range. Therefore, it's critical to provide correct, adequately heated or cooled conditions for snakes. Gerry checks the external temperature near one of the cages. "A hundred and six degrees [Fahrenheit]," he says, looking at the temperature. "That's way too much. No snake will live in that."

Clue number two is found in the glass enclosures where the snakes lived. Gerry climbs in through one of the windows to take a closer look at the inside. He's not satisfied at all with what he finds. As he looks around the tiny living unit, he notices electrical wiring near the top of the wall. "Okay. To start with," he explains, "you never want any electric wiring anywhere here. It's just too dangerous for snakes."

Clue number three lies just beneath Gerry's feet as he inspects the units. He reaches down and picks up the sand that covers the floor and lets it run through his fingers. He then takes a moment to examine the traces of sand left on his hands. As he does, one can see the look of disgust on his face. "The sand is way too fine. It's just like dust, and that's not good. Infections just swell out of it." It's not a surprise that the snakes became ill and died in this environment.

After his examination of the facility, Gerry takes note of all the issues in order to submit a report to the sheikh and Muhammad. It's clear that the enclosures are the primary source of most of the problems. A secondary cause of the issues could be the staff of the facility itself. Gerry explains: "From speaking with the park staff and looking at these enclosures, the enclosures played a big role in the cause of death for all these snakes here. So we're going to have to change [the enclosures] and then change the way they've been dealing with the snakes because they were taught wrong. And that should be fine. We can get new snakes and keep them happy and alive."

After the inspection, Gerry provides a report detailing his findings explicitly, which includes suggestions for repairs to the enclosures. As he does so, he details the issues around the park that need to be amended. "[There are] some places where the **tin**[8] roof has come off the wall, so there's the **gap**[9] there," he explains before continuing to the next point. Now that Gerry's highlighted the problems and solved the case, it's time for Muhammad and him to take action.

---

[8]**tin:** a grayish, flexible, metal
[9]**gap:** space between two things

Identify Cause and Effect

Identify three possible causes of death for the snakes from page 11.

First on the list in order to make a proper home for the snakes is to restore and rebuild the park—and that means disposing of the old materials and replacing them with appropriate ones. Gerry and Muhammad leave in the snake park's truck to shop for materials and supplies to equip the enclosures. These new supplies will be essential in ensuring the snakes' survival. Gerry buys plants and trees to make the living environments more appropriate for the snakes. He also buys a special type of carpet-like material that will protect the snakes from the heat of the external environment.

The next item that must be addressed is finding the correct foods for the snakes, and Gerry knows what's number one on the menu for most of them. "You have a pet store here, no?" he asks Muhammad. The two men go to the store and buy some mice—a favorite food for many snakes. As he closes up the box full of mice, Gerry can't help but joke and say "Happy snakes!" as he prepares to take the mice back for his favorite animals.

Finally, Gerry and Muhammad return to the snake park and unpack the truck. At this point, the snake detective takes a moment to report on the progress of the park repairs. "We've got just about everything we need to redo the enclosures right now," says Gerry. "Plants, food, rocks, **matting**,[10] **foam**[11]—just about everything that we could possibly need to make this a good place for snakes."

---

[10] **matting:** a rough material for covering floors
[11] **foam:** a soft light rubber material

It's crucial that the park's restoration is successful so that the next shipment of snakes will not only survive, they'll do well. The park cannot afford any more mistakes as a new bunch of snakes is on its way. Two days later, Gerry hears the word that the snake shipment has reached Oman. At last, Gerry will have a chance to see if all of his hard work has paid off and if he's made an environment in which the new snakes can live. "We have the snakes," he says happily as he goes to prepare for the arrival of the new shipment.

It's nighttime when the new residents get to the park. The snakes may have arrived, but Gerry has no idea whether or not all of them have survived their journey. The wooden boxes need to be opened fast to make sure the new arrivals are alive and well. Gerry starts to work on unpacking the shipment of snakes, which includes a dangerous green mamba. Africa's green mamba is one of the most venomous snakes in the world, and unfortunately, the shipment doesn't come with antivenom. Gerry has to be especially cautious with this one. One wrong move and the snake could bite him and, without antivenom, the bite could be deadly.

Sequence the Events

What is the correct order of the events? Write numbers.

_____ Gerry and Muhammad buy food for the snakes.

_____ They open the wooden boxes containing the snakes.

_____ They buy plants and trees for the park.

_____ The shipment of new snakes arrives.

_____ They unpack the supplies from the truck.

As Gerry moves through the piles of boxes and examines them, he pauses before opening the one with the mambas in it. Finally, he works the box open and gently lifts one of the heavy bags. "The mamba's a snake that scares me," says Gerry. "And there [are] four of them in this bag." He goes on to explain how to handle these dangerous reptiles safely. "You always want to keep in mind to hold the snake bag above the **knot**.[12] You never want to grab it [down] there or rest it on your lap or sling it over your shoulder. So many snake handlers—good snake handlers—have actually gotten bitten that way. You never **take a snake for granted**."[13]

While park staff members watch nervously nearby, Gerry releases one of the thin green snakes. It moves amazingly fast, but luckily Gerry does too. He quickly picks the snake up by the tail and gently slings the snake over a long, hooked metal stick used for catching snakes. As he handles the snake, he talks about the nature of the dangerous beauties: "The mambas are incredibly fast snakes, probably the most feared snakes in the world, and rightly so. They can move so fast, and they're so slender. It's amazing." Gerry continues to manipulate the snake around the metal stick, always keeping one move ahead of the animal. As he does, he notes, "This snake could kill me," but then adds, "but, she's not going to," as he quickly moves the reptile over to its new home. There's one uncomfortable moment at the door of the cage when the snake extends itself back out towards Gerry. Gerry, however, is too quick for the animal and manages to safely constrain it in its new home.

---

[12] **knot:** a tied point
[13] **take (something) for granted:** be so used to something that one doesn't recognize its true value, danger, or other quality

It's late in the evening at this point, but somehow working with the snakes has made Gerry feel wide awake and lively. "I was tired," he reports, "but now with these snakes, I'm just feeling alive again." In just a few hours, Gerry safely places two dozen deadly snakes into their new enclosures. He manages to do so without a single bite. Muhammad, however, isn't so lucky. While Gerry is handling a small red snake, the snake strikes out and bites Muhammad. Luckily, the snake is harmless. Muhammad quickly puts his finger in his mouth and sucks on his finger. Surprisingly, he then holds the flame from his lighter over the wound. As he does so, he explains the purpose of this step, "[It's] to release the pain of snake." At last, he relaxes with a smile and says, "It's okay." It seems that Muhammad's painful meeting with his new resident turned out to be all right after all.

The snake park team is getting down to the last boxes. As they do, Gerry picks up a small blue cloth bag and then raises his eyebrows in surprise when he sees the label. "Ah-ha!" he says and carefully puts the bag on the ground. "Oh, I do not believe this. I do not believe this," says Gerry excitedly, as the snake is released. To an Indian herpetologist who came into contact with a lot of cobras as he was growing up, the snake that he is so excited about is actually a fairly common one from the western part of the U.S. and Mexico: a rattlesnake.

As Gerry stands there looking at the animal in amazement, it starts to shake its noisy rattle to make a sharp noise. "I have never heard the rattle of a live rattlesnake before," he reports. For a herpetologist, it's always exciting to have contact with a new type of snake. He takes a good look at the animal, and then gently encourages it to relax. "Okay, okay, calm down. Easy does it," he says as he prepares to move the dangerous snake. "Who would imagine I would come to Oman and then see a rattlesnake here?" he declares at last. Finally, Gerry picks up the rattlesnake and moves it to its new home. "[I'm going to] lock it up real[ly] good," he says. "We don't want rattlesnakes getting loose in Oman!"

It's the early hours of the morning by the time the snakes are all safely enclosed in their new homes. "Well, it's four-thirty in the morning," reports Gerry. "We've put all the snakes in their enclosures and tomorrow we have to see that they've settled in well." The next day, Gerry will start working with Muhammad to make sure that he really knows how to handle the new snakes. This is especially important, as Muhammad will be Gerry's successor for caring for the snakes when Gerry leaves. "We start handling them tomorrow," he says to the general manager. "You and I can work with them and [I'll] show you what has to be fed to what and how to play with them and how to deal with them." But Gerry has something else on his mind right now. "Let's try to get some sleep," he says to Muhammad as he says good night and heads off to bed.

The two men spend the next two weeks working extremely hard, cleaning, training, and preparing for the opening day of the park. At last the day arrives and the doors are opened as the first new visitors come in: a group of adults and children who are all thrilled to be able to see the **exotic**[14] snakes. As they enter the park, the visitors are greeted by the staff. One can see the delight in the children's eyes when they are given the chance to actually hold some of the non-venomous snakes.

As for the general manager Muhammad, he has acquired new skills and now has new snakes to look after. He's busy rebuilding his dream of being a snake handler. Having learned so much from Gerry, he's also enjoying his chance to teach others about snakes. He confidently shows guest after guest how to handle the snakes properly, and then hands each snake over with a big smile once the guest consents to hold it. To one guest who is curious about why Muhammad is so good with the snakes, he simply replies, "I like them. That's why they like me."

---

[14]**exotic:** unusual and attractive, especially from other countries

For the sheikh, asking Gerry to intervene in the park was money well spent because now the snake park is operating again—this time correctly. This is Oman's first snake park, and it's important to everyone involved with the park that it's a success. As he watches the first visitors enjoy the park, Gerry explains why these parks are a good idea. "[One of] the most important things that snake parks achieve is actually giving people a firsthand experience with snakes. And that includes letting them hold a snake now and then to **debunk the myths**[15] that they're **slimy**[6] and aggressive and all they really want to do is harm us. But you can't really tell a person that unless they actually experience that for themselves."

Thanks to Gerry Martin, visitors to Oman's first snake park are getting an opportunity to actually see and touch snakes for themselves. They're also getting a chance to learn more—and learn the truth—about these animals that are so often misjudged by humans. It looks like the 'snake detective' has successfully solved the snake mystery of Oman.

---

[15]**debunk (a) myth:** show that a commonly believed idea is false
[16]**slimy:** having an unpleasant, wet feel

Snake parks give people firsthand experience with snakes.

Summarize

Imagine that you are a newspaper or radio reporter in Oman. Write or tell the story of Gerry Martin and the snake park. Include the following information:

1. Why did the sheikh call in a foreign expert?

2. How did Gerry Martin begin his investigation?

3. What solutions did he find to the mystery, and how did he solve the problems?

After You Read

1. What is Gerry most concerned about when he talks to Sheikh Amer al-Suleimani on the phone?
   A. what kind of currency Oman uses
   B. how many snakes the sheikh has
   C. why so many snakes have died
   D. what kind of new snakes the sheikh will get

2. What point does the writer make about the sheikh on page 7?
   A. He feels frustrated.
   B. He is to blame for the dead snakes.
   C. He cares about people, not snakes.
   D. He gets sad very easily.

3. What's unusual about the snake described on page 7?
   A. It's a python.
   B. It's yellow.
   C. It's slung over the shoulder of a park employee.
   D. It's the park's only remaining snake.

4. What is implied about the Southeast Asian snake experts?
   A. They committed an offense.
   B. They were comprehensive.
   C. They acted morally.
   D. They were only volunteers.

5. All of the following are areas where Gerry finds a problem in the snake enclosures EXCEPT:
   A. the temperatures
   B. the electrical wiring
   C. the glass fronts
   D. the sand

6. The word 'lies' in paragraph 3 on page 11 can be replaced by:
   A. deviates
   B. speaks untruthfully
   C. arises
   D. is present

7. What is the main purpose of the shopping trip described on page 15?
   A. to replace the glass fronts on the enclosures
   B. to prepare the park for the arrival of new snakes
   C. to get food supplies for the albino python
   D. to get plants for Muhammad's office

8. Which of the following is a suitable heading for paragraph 2 on page 16?
   A. Snakes Depart at Night
   B. Reptiles Suffer During Journey
   C. Shipment Lacks Antivenom
   D. Green Mamba Attacks!

9. According to Gerry, why do many good snake handlers get bitten?
   A. They forget to be careful when handling the snakes.
   B. They knot the bag incorrectly.
   C. They don't know that mambas are deadly.
   D. They carry the snakes in a box, not a bag.

10. One reason Gerry gets so excited to see a rattlesnake is:
   A. It's such a common snake.
   B. He is not from the U.S. or Mexico.
   C. It's his favorite kind of snake.
   D. It's the most dangerous snake in the world.

11. Muhammad shows visitors his impressive skill _____ snakes.
   A. for
   B. to
   C. of
   D. with

12. Which of these statements best summarizes the reason for having a snake park?
   A. Snake parks spread ignorance about snakes.
   B. Snakes can scare people.
   C. The public gets an education about snakes.
   D. Visitors can have a wilderness experience.

Gerry Martin: The Reptile Man

A Born Snake Lover

Born in Ahmedabad, India, in 1975, Gerry Martin developed a great interest in nature at a very early age. He became particularly interested in wild animals, such as snakes and reptiles. While most people are not very attracted to this type of wildlife, Martin always had an intense fascination. According to one report, when he was three years old, he apparently jumped into the python pit of a snake park in India. His mother also says that Gerry was constantly bringing home all sorts of animals when he was young. However, Gerry's interests do not extend to all of the Martins. In the same article, the herpetologist notes that no one else in his family shares his great love of snakes.

The Interest Grows

Martin's interest in reptiles continued to grow and by the age of 17 he had already started assisting Romulus Whitaker at the Madras Crocodile Bank. The goal of this agency is to ensure the survival of this endangered animal in India. In 1996, Martin became the youngest curator, or manager, to be entrusted with this important position. Since then, Martin has continued to do important research in the field of herpetology and has served as an expert advisor on a wide variety of National Geographic documentaries. He has also appeared on screen in the National Geographic Channel movies 'Wild Things' and 'World Gone Wild.' Meanwhile, he continues to develop the academic side of his career. He is busy creating a comprehensive listing of reptiles in India, which he hopes future generations of herpetologists will find useful in their conservation efforts.

Educational Opportunities in Herpetology

Schools	Local Educational Support	Other Program Advantages	Degrees Offered
University of Florida	Florida Integrated Science Center; Florida Museum of Natural History	opportunities to observe research at the Archie Carr National Wildlife Refuge	Bachelor's, Master's, and Ph.D. in herpetology
University of Texas, Arlington	Amphibian and Reptile Diversity Research Center collection	professors often do research in Central America, South America, Africa, and Asia	Master's in biology with a thesis option in herpetology
Russian Academy of Sciences, St. Petersburg, Russia	the university's herpetology collection of over 22,000 reptiles	expedition opportunities to Kazakhstan, Uzbekistan, Tajikistan, and Kyrgyzstan	extensive coursework and herpetology research opportunities offered

Helping People Help Reptiles

Because of his devotion to conserving and restoring the world's reptile population, Martin understands how crucial it is to educate young people. He does this primarily through camps and other educational programs. Martin provides children with an extraordinary experience by taking groups into India's countryside where they camp out for several days, observing the local reptile population up close. They learn how to identify various snakes and even get an opportunity to learn safe handling techniques. In addition, as part of an Education Outreach Program organized by National Geographic, Martin has also traveled to several countries in Southeast Asia presenting programs to young people about the importance of reptile conservation. This work, in combination with his academic research, has made Gerry Martin one of the world's most extraordinary herpetologists.

CD 2, Track 04

Word Count: 401
Time: _____

Vocabulary List

albino python (3, 7)
antivenom (2, 16)
clue (2, 4, 11)
cobra (3, 20)
debunk (a) myth (26)
enclosure (7, 11, 12, 15, 20, 23)
exotic (24)
foam (15)
gap (12)
grab (8, 19)
green mamba (3, 16, 19)
herpetologist (2, 4, 20, 23)
knot (19)
matting (15)
noose (8)
rattlesnake (3, 20, 23)
reptile (2, 7, 8, 19)
sheikh (4, 7, 8, 12, 26, 27)
slimy (26)
sling (7, 19)
take (something) for granted (19)
tin (12)
venomous (2, 16, 24)

Metric Conversion Chart

Area
1 hectare = 2.471 acres

Length
1 centimeter = .394 inches
1 meter = 1.094 yards
1 kilometer = .621 miles

Temperature
0° Celsius = 32° Fahrenheit

Volume
1 liter = 1.057 quarts

Weight
1 gram = .035 ounces
1 kilogram = 2.2 pounds